A Silvey-Jex

BAD TASTE BOOK

To ....

From...

FROM BEGINNING TO END

Published in Great Britain by Silvey-Jex Publications

Printed in England by Merlin Colour Printers, Canvey Island, Essex.

"Which one of them is my husband?"

"I don't suppose you've noticed I'm pregnant?"

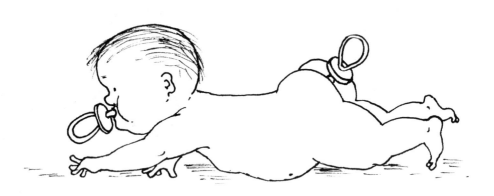

"Well he was born with them on – so I don't like to take them off"

"It's a bloody **high,** high chair isn't it?"

"Let's get married and make babies you said"

"He's going to be tall isn't he?"

"I think you should have tried the little fellow on the potty first."

"Aaahh . . . he's the image of you Lil"

"Wait . . . here he is . . . no . . . yes . . . oops . . . try again"

"Yes . . . Doctor said he was a bit premature"

" . . .but spots are part of growing up dear"

"Salt – Mustard – Vinegar – Schoolboys"

" . . . and then the wind changed"

"Morning Head"

"He's upset because there's no glue in it"

"Hello Sailor"

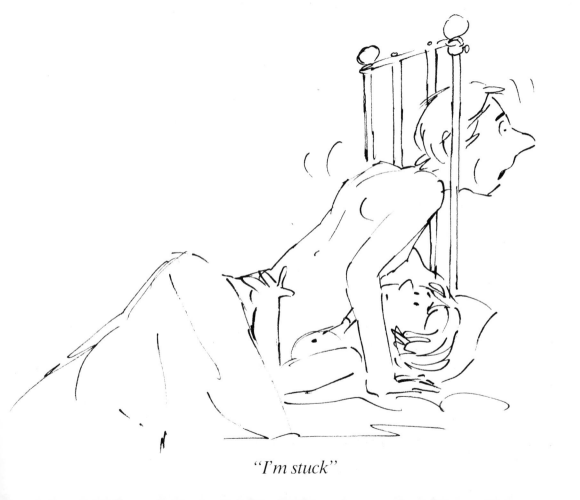

"I'm stuck"

"Oh yes, definitely with my body I thee worship . . ."

"Tell me Doctor – how long before rigor-mortis sets in?"

"Went to a wife swapping party last night – swapped the wife for a set of socket spanners"

"What do you want. Jam – honey – fishpaste – middle aged spread?"

*"For God's sake Richard stop making a fuss
or the Robinsons will think you didn't enjoy the meal."*

"His last words were 'I've decided to take up jogging''

"Oh Mr. Jenkins, I expect you think I'm awful"

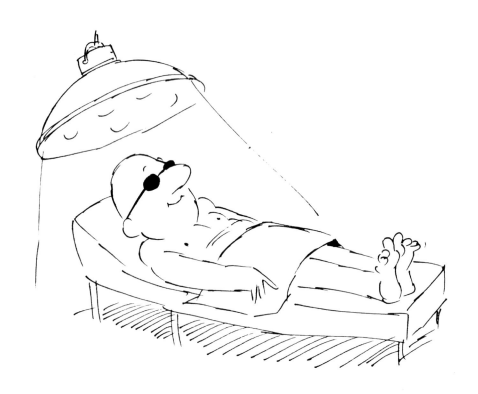

"Your trouble is sex and drugs and rock 'n roll . . . why not try some?"

"This isn't a first class season . . . it's a death certificate"

Bernard Hardcastle, being of sound mind tweedly diddle oh pom pom poo . . .”

"*Whatever it is you're doing – stop it*"

"Doctor can see you now"

"After you with the bottle ... I'm bursting."

"And now something appropriate from the Ancient and Modern"

"My, my, we're slow today Mr. Hoskins."

"Down, you bugger, down"

"Good Heavens look at that – a Charlie Chaplin cane"

"If its alright with you Mr. Plumpton...
I like a second opinion."

"Well Doctor . . . how long have I got?"

"Trousers Mr Thompson ... trousers."

"Geoffry's gone punk... he's got his collar stud through his nose."

"Hmm…and you say he was alright yesterday"?

"Doctor sent me to do a death mask"

"*Must go now Mother, George has just died*"

"*Harry always was a flash bugger wasn't he?*"

"Yes, Mary Ford, beloved wife .. devoted mother of ten .. widow .. this is your .."

"I don't know about you but I'm dead on my feet"

"Grandad always loved Guy Fawkes night"

"I've found your heart pills at last dear, they were in the . . . oh?"

"I'd have thought that even 'economy' would have warrented a box"

"Aahh just look at him. That week in Blackpool did him the power of good"

"Old Ted seems to be taking it well"

"Excuse me . . . has anybody got a light?"

"Of course, I was with him when he went you know"

"Until now . . . I'd never believed in levitation"

"Didn't you once work as a coalman?"

"Is this him?"

"Go easy with him lads, this is his first Post-Mortem"

"It's no good, I can't take him seriously when he wears his glasses"

"Remember the old saying . . . 'fools rush in where angels fear to tread'?"

"Well . . . it's just that I imagined you sort of bigger somehow"

"I thought we'd seen the last of that sort of thing."

"If I'd known they were like that I would have come here sooner?"

"He'll kill himself one of these days"

"Where the Hell have you been?"

"We crashed on the way to the cemetary"

Also published by Silvey-Jex Publications
BAD TASTE BOOKS
including
TOILET HUMOUR, GERIATRICS, ILLNESS, BOGIES.
TOILET HUMOUR NO 2, WILDLIFE, SNOWMEN, FLASHERS.
CHRISTMAS

BOY AND GIRL

SNAILSBURY TALES